Great Artists

Rembrandt

Adam G. Klein

ABDO
Publishing Company

Published by ABDO Publishing Company, 4940 Viking Drive, Edina, Minnesota 55435.
Copyright © 2007 by Abdo Consulting Group, Inc. International copyrights reserved in all
countries. No part of this book may be reproduced in any form without written permission from
the publisher. The Checkerboard Library™ is a trademark and logo of ABDO Publishing
Company.

Printed in the United States.

Cover Photo: Corbis
Interior Photos: Art Resource pp. 1, 5, 12, 15, 17, 21; Bridgeman Art Library pp. 9, 11, 13, 16,
   23, 27; Corbis pp. 19, 23, 25, 29; Getty Images pp. 15, 28

Series Coordinator: Megan M. Gunderson
Editors: Megan M. Gunderson, Megan Murphy
Cover Design: Neil Klinepier
Interior Design: Dave Bullen

Library of Congress Cataloging-in-Publication Data

Klein, Adam G., 1976-
  Rembrandt / Adam G. Klein.
    p. cm. -- (Great artists)
  Includes index.
  ISBN-10 1-59679-735-5
  ISBN-13 978-1-59679-735-2
  1. Rembrandt Harmenszoon van Rijn, 1606-1669--Juvenile literature. 2. Artists--Netherlands--
Biography--Juvenile literature. I. Rembrandt Harmenszoon van Rijn, 1606-1669. II. Title III.
Series: Klein, Adam G., 1976- . Great artists.

N6953.R4K54 2006
759.9492--dc22
                                                                              2005017893

Contents

Rembrandt

Rembrandt Harmenszoon van Rijn is considered one of the greatest Dutch painters. He is known for his talent in a variety of artistic **genres**. In the 1600s, many Dutch painters focused on **still lifes** and scenes of daily life. But Rembrandt also painted dramatic scenes from history, mythology, and the Bible. And, he created more than 80 self-portraits.

During his lifetime, Rembrandt became an influential artist. He had natural talent and quickly rose to fame. He gained popularity by painting portraits for important customers. Rembrandt felt he had nothing to worry about. But, he found this was not true. He fell from prosperity as quickly as he had risen to fame.

Throughout his career, Rembrandt's style was distinctive. His dramatic figures and energetic brushstrokes created a whole new look in art. Whether he was prosperous or not, Rembrandt's art always showed skill and emotion. Rembrandt was an artist who changed the world.

Rembrandt painted Self-Portrait at the Age of 23 in 1629.

This painting from 1669 is one of Rembrandt's final self-portraits.

Timeline

1606 ~ On July 15, Rembrandt Harmenszoon van Rijn was born in Leiden, Netherlands.

1619 to 1622 ~ Rembrandt was apprenticed to Jacob Isaacszoon van Swanenburg.

1623 ~ For six months, Rembrandt was apprenticed to Pieter Lastman.

1625 ~ Rembrandt painted *Stoning of St. Stephen*.

1633 ~ Rembrandt created *The Shipbuilder Jan Rijcksen and His Wife Griet Jans* and *The Storm on the Sea of Galilee*.

1635 ~ Rembrandt painted *Rembrandt and Saskia as the Prodigal Son*.

1636 ~ Rembrandt completed *The Blinding of Samson*.

1638 ~ Rembrandt sketched *The Actor Who Played the Role of Bishop Gosewijn*.

1640 to 1642 ~ Rembrandt painted his largest work, the *Night Watch*.

1643 ~ Rembrandt etched the *Three Trees*.

1661 ~ Rembrandt painted *The Conspiracy of the Batavians Under Claudius Civilis*.

1669 ~ Rembrandt died on October 4.

Fun Facts

- Throughout his life, Rembrandt collected items for inspiration. He had a room in his house filled with glassware, seashells, and corals. There were also globes, unusual weapons, and statues of Roman emperors. But, Rembrandt's favorite possessions were his art books. In these books, he kept about 8,000 drawings and prints by famous artists.

- Rembrandt had an oak press in his home that he used to produce his etchings. To create an etching, Rembrandt ran an inked plate through the wooden press with a moist sheet of paper. He then hung the finished etching on a line to dry.

- Several of Rembrandt's most famous works are group portraits. Typically, figures in a group portrait were placed in a line so that each person could be seen properly. However, Rembrandt did not follow this rule in the *Night Watch* or the *Syndics of the Drapers' Guild*. Instead, his paintings portray people more naturally. They often appear to capture a single moment in time.

Early Education

Rembrandt Harmenszoon van Rijn was born on July 15, 1606, in Leiden, Netherlands. He was the ninth child of Harmen Gerritszoon van Rijn and Neeltje van Zuytbroeck. Rembrandt's mother came from a family of bakers. Harmen owned a mill, which helped support his large family.

Rembrandt's family had enough money to send him to a good school. So from 1615 to 1619, Rembrandt attended the Leiden Latin School. There, he studied mathematics, mythology, Latin, and the Bible. Then he **enrolled** at Leiden University, the first university in the Netherlands.

However, Rembrandt decided he did not want to be a scholar. He wanted to be an artist. Being an artist was a good career, so Rembrandt's parents supported his decision. They arranged for him to become an **apprentice** to Jacob Isaacszoon van Swanenburg.

Rembrandt was Van Swanenburg's **apprentice** from 1619 to 1622. In Leiden, Rembrandt's skills improved quickly. His father agreed that it would be best for Rembrandt to continue his education in a larger city. So in 1623, Rembrandt headed to Amsterdam, Netherlands, for more training.

Many of the older men and women in Rembrandt's portraits have been identified as his parents.

Amsterdam

In Amsterdam, Rembrandt became an **apprentice** to Pieter Lastman. But after just six months, Rembrandt decided to work on his own. He returned to Leiden to paint.

In Leiden, Rembrandt created paintings based on history, mythology, and the Bible. Many people were interested in works on those subjects. One of Rembrandt's first professional paintings was **commissioned** by an important Leiden citizen, Petrus Scriverius. *Stoning of St. Stephen* was completed in 1625.

To save money, Rembrandt shared studio space with an artist named Jan Lievens. They worked together and helped each other with their careers. In fact, they often created works on the same theme as a kind of competition. This friendly rivalry helped each artist improve his **technique**.

By the late 1620s, Rembrandt's work had gained him many admirers. Constantijn Huygens was one of his earliest **patrons**.

Stoning of St. Stephen *is Rembrandt's first dated work.*

Huygens was impressed with Rembrandt's ability to show emotion in his paintings. With his reputation spreading, Rembrandt felt it was time to return to Amsterdam.

Portrait Painting

In 1631, Rembrandt left Leiden. His art dealer, Hendrick Uylenburgh, made the move easier. Uylenburgh let Rembrandt live in his home in Amsterdam. And, he gave Rembrandt studio space. With all his needs met, Rembrandt began painting.

Rembrandt soon became known for his portraits. He painted *The Shipbuilder Jan Rijcksen and His Wife Griet Jans* in 1633. This work shows a husband and wife in the same painting. It is one of Rembrandt's few double portraits.

Word spread quickly about Rembrandt's special talent. He became one of the most popular and well-paid portrait artists in Amsterdam. Rembrandt had about 50 portrait

Rembrandt drew this sketch of Saskia three days after they became engaged.

commissions during his first four years there. He also completed a biblical painting titled *The Storm on the Sea of Galilee* in 1633.

Despite his busy schedule, Rembrandt found time to enjoy his success. On June 22, 1634, he married Uylenburgh's cousin Saskia. She was the daughter of a wealthy family from Leeuwarden, Netherlands. Rembrandt rented a home, and the **newlyweds** began their life together.

Thieves stole The Storm on the Sea of Galilee *from the* Isabella Stewart Gardner Museum in Boston, Massachusetts, in 1990.

Enjoying Success

In just a few years, Rembrandt had reached the top of his profession. He enjoyed his success and became accustomed to expensive things. In 1635, Rembrandt painted a view of his life. *Rembrandt and Saskia as the Prodigal Son* is the largest self-portrait Rembrandt created. This image shows Rembrandt enjoying an evening out with his wife.

In 1636, he painted *The Blinding of Samson*. This work highlighted Rembrandt's growing talent for **chiaroscuro**. However, it was so realistically unsettling that Rembrandt had difficulty selling it. Huygens refused to accept it as a gift, but Rembrandt sent it to him anyway.

Despite this incident, Rembrandt had many successful paintings. His work was in high demand. People waited years for their paintings to be finished. And Rembrandt found other ways to expand his business. If a painting was popular, he created prints of it to sell. And for a fee, he taught students in his studio.

Artist's Corner

Rembrandt

Rembrandt is known for his self-portraits. They are special, because viewers can watch him age over time. Rembrandt painted self-portraits from his early years as an artist until the year of his death. In this way, scholars also have a record of his changing artistic styles. The self-portrait genre allowed Rembrandt to experiment with styles, facial expressions, poses, and costumes. He did just that in *Rembrandt and Saskia as the Prodigal Son (left)*.

In the Netherlands, many artists also created tronies. *Tronies* is Dutch for "heads." These small works were often used as practice. They are not considered official portraits. Tronies simply represent a variety of facial expressions and costumes. However, some of Rembrandt's self-portraits are considered tronies *(right)*. And, the genre became a popular style to collect.

A New Subject

Besides painting, Rembrandt had other interests, such as theater. Because he liked plays, Rembrandt sometimes drew actors. He sketched *The Actor Who Played the Role of Bishop Gosewijn* in 1638. Rembrandt studied the emotions of actors. He could then use these in his own work.

Despite his success, Rembrandt's private life was sometimes difficult. Saskia's family often complained that the **newlyweds** were spending too much money. Rembrandt had become wealthy quickly, and he and Saskia spent freely. So, Saskia's family threatened to cut off her inheritance. But, Rembrandt **sued** her family for the money and won.

Rembrandt studied the costumes and poses of actors.

As Titus grew, Rembrandt portrayed him several times. Like many of his models, Rembrandt often painted Titus wearing costumes.

Rembrandt felt his future looked great. In 1639, he bought a large house. After settling into his new surroundings, Rembrandt had more good news. In September 1641, Saskia gave birth to their son, Titus. Rembrandt had a new subject to paint. So, he began creating pictures of family life.

Night Watch

Around the time Titus was born, Rembrandt was **commissioned** to create his largest work. From 1640 to 1642, Rembrandt painted the *Night Watch* for a company of soldiers.

This important project was a great honor. Sixteen soldiers and two commanders paid a considerable fee to have the group portrait created. In it, Captain Frans Banning Cocq and Lieutenant Willem van Ruytenburgh are surrounded by their men. Other people were added to the picture to make it look full and active.

Dutch soldiers hired several artists to create a total of six paintings for the project. The works were to be hung in their new meeting hall. Many of the influential people in Amsterdam would see them. This was a chance for Rembrandt to show off his skills in a highly visible space.

But Rembrandt's excitement over the project did not last long. Saskia died on June 14, 1642, around the time the *Night Watch* was completed. In her will, all of her money was left to take care

The Night Watch *is now housed in the Rijksmuseum in Amsterdam.*

of Titus. If Rembrandt decided to remarry, he would lose half of everything he owned. To add to this tragedy, Rembrandt's relationship with Uylenburgh soured. This would make finding future work difficult.

Changes

When the *Night Watch* was put on display, there were various reactions to the work. Most viewers were used to group portraits with the subjects lined up. In the *Night Watch*, Rembrandt didn't even make all the faces completely visible. So, some people thought it was too dark and **chaotic**. Still, others thought the large painting had energy and realism.

The *Night Watch* marks a turning point in Rembrandt's life. People's tastes had changed, and they were not as interested in the kind of work Rembrandt was creating. Rembrandt still had **patrons**, but many were of a lower **status** in his community.

To earn money, he continued teaching other artists. But, some of his former students were getting better **commissions** than he was! And even though Rembrandt wasn't earning as much money, he continued to spend freely. Soon, he began having financial difficulties.

The **Three Trees** *combines stormy skies, bold chiaroscuro, and a rural Dutch setting in one etching.*

In the 1640s, Rembrandt changed his style. His brushstrokes and his use of **chiaroscuro** became bolder. He also began drawing and etching views of the city and the countryside. He had painted dramatic landscapes earlier, but his new works focused more on local Dutch scenes. The *Three Trees* etching, from 1643, combines all of these elements.

Troubles

Even with Rembrandt's style changes, some people remained loyal to him. One of his most supportive remaining **patrons** was Jan Six, a high-ranking member of society. Over the years, Six bought existing paintings and **commissioned** new works.

During the 1640s, Rembrandt had been dating Titus's nurse, Geertghe Dircx. This relationship failed. And in 1647, he started dating Hendrickje Stoffels. Dircx was furious, so she **sued** Rembrandt. He had to pay her an allowance, which added to his already troubled finances.

Eventually, Rembrandt found out that Dircx was stealing from him. So, he paid to put her in an institution. None of this helped Rembrandt's money problems. He had not finished paying for his house. And, people were starting to ask him to pay his **debts**. In 1653, Rembrandt tried to collect money from people who owed him, but it was not enough.

Changing Styles

While Rembrandt's artwork remained popular, his painting style did not always follow the accepted rules. The shifting style of Rembrandt's artwork can be seen in his portrait commissions. Early in his career, portraits such as A Lady and Gentleman in Black (detail, left) were refined and highly detailed. The woman's collar, the lace on her sleeve, and the design on her dress are realistic.

But in later years, Rembrandt experimented more with his brushwork. So, his work sometimes appears unfinished or unrefined. His portrait of Jan Six (right) is an early example of this. Rembrandt's brushstrokes are broad, especially on Six's clothing. Still, they remain as precise as the brushstrokes in his earlier works. Six was a fan of this experimental brushwork, though many people were not.

The Solution

In 1655, Rembrandt tried to buy a smaller house so he could pay his **debts**. But, no one would loan him money for a new home. So, Rembrandt **auctioned** off many paintings and much of what he owned. Yet he still did not have enough money. In 1656, Rembrandt lost his house and declared **bankruptcy**.

The same year, Titus and Stoffels created an art dealership. They gave Rembrandt a salary and sold his work. This way, Rembrandt would not live in poverty. Many people disapproved of Rembrandt's relationship with Stoffels and his bankruptcy. Even Six stopped hiring him. Still, Rembrandt continued to get a few jobs.

Around this time, Rembrandt felt free to paint the way that he wanted. His previous work was typically polished and realistic. Now, his paintings seemed less finished. But, they gained a new kind of emotion. Rembrandt showed his feelings through his brushstrokes. No one had ever seen anything like it before.

In 1656, Rembrandt's possessions were inventoried because of his bankruptcy. Historians used this list of belongings to help restore his house to look like it did during his lifetime.

The Town Hall

Rembrandt continued to challenge popular styles of art. And despite his previous troubles, he was still highly regarded as an artist. In 1661, Rembrandt was **commissioned** to create a painting for the new town hall in Amsterdam. He was one of several artists hired to participate in this large, important project.

All the paintings commissioned for the town hall were to be scenes of the Batavians. More than a thousand years earlier, the Batavians had fought against the Roman Empire. Rembrandt painted *The Conspiracy of the Batavians Under Claudius Civilis*. This painting was 20 feet (6 m) tall and 18 feet (5 m) wide. It celebrated the independence of the Netherlands.

In 1662, the painting was accepted. But Rembrandt was never paid for it, and it was later returned to him. Some scholars think the figures in *The Conspiracy* may have seemed too uncivilized for the town hall project. Others believe Rembrandt simply didn't accept the price offered for the work.

When The Conspiracy of the Batavians Under Claudius Civilis *was removed from the town hall, another artist's work took its place. In order to sell his work, Rembrandt cut the painting to make it smaller.*

National Treasure

To continue earning money, Rembrandt kept working with students. Many of them respected his work and several became famous themselves. Still, teaching fees did not pay Rembrandt enough. Then in July 1663, Stoffels died.

In time, Rembrandt's family grew again. Titus married Magdalena van Loo in February 1668. Unfortunately, Titus died in September of that year. But his daughter, Titia, was born in March 1669. Rembrandt became one of her guardians. But he did not get to spend much time with Titia. Rembrandt died the following autumn on October 4, 1669.

Rembrandt's work was featured on the cover of Time *magazine on November 24, 1961.*

Historians know Rembrandt was buried in the Westerkerk, a church in Amsterdam, but his grave was unmarked.

After Rembrandt's death, people continued to appreciate his work. For hundreds of years, artists have looked to Rembrandt's paintings for inspiration. The home that Rembrandt lost is now the Rembrandt House Museum. Today, Rembrandt is a national treasure in the Netherlands.

Glossary

apprentice - a person who learns a trade or a craft from a skilled worker.

auction - a public sale at which goods are sold to the highest bidder.

bankrupt - legally declared unable to pay debts.

chaotic - of or relating to a state of total confusion.

chiaroscuro - the arrangement and contrast of light and dark, often used to increase the emotion or drama of a work of art.

commission - a request to complete a work, such as a painting, for a certain person. To be commissioned is to be given such a request.

debt - something owed to someone, usually money.

enroll - to register, especially in order to attend a school.

genre - a category of art, music, or literature.

newlywed - a person who just married.

patron - one who supports an individual or a cause with money, resources, or influence.

status - a position or rank in a social or professional standing.

still life - a painting or a picture made up of nonmoving objects.

sue - to bring a person or an organization to court.

technique - a method or style in which something is done.

Saying It

chiaroscuro - kee-ahr-uh-SKYUR-oh
Constantijn Huygens - KAWN-stahn-tine HUHIH-kuhns
Hendrick Uylenburgh - HEHN-druhk OY-luhm-boork
Jan Lievens - YAHN LEE vuhns
Leeuwarden - LAY-vahr-duh
Leiden - LIED-uhn

Web Sites

To learn more about Rembrandt, visit ABDO Publishing Company on the World Wide Web at **www.abdopublishing.com**. Web sites about Rembrandt are featured on our Book Links page. These links are routinely monitored and updated to provide the most current information available.

Index